*let me straighten your crown, queen*

*Journals by Amity*

*Copyright © 2022*

# let me straighten your crown, queen

A POCKET-SIZED
BOOK OF AFFIRMATIONS
TO RECENTER THE ROYALTY IN
YOU

I am
*Divine*
child

I am
*really*
real

FEEL YOUR
*body*

GIVE.
SHARE.
LOVE.

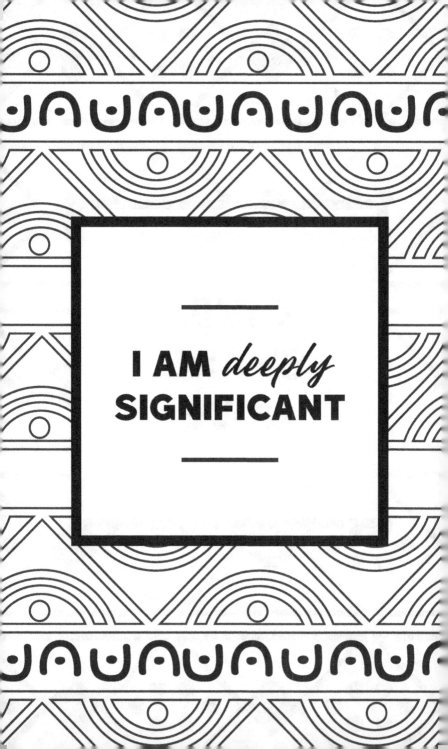

# Listen to your
*inner-child*

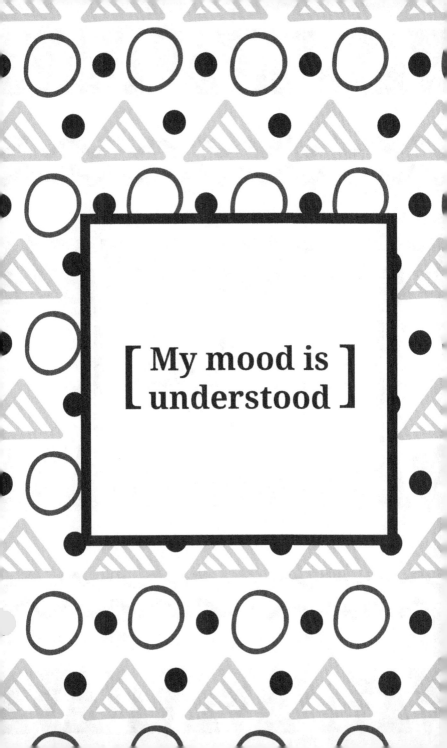

[ My mood is ]
[ understood ]

**LIVE IN THE PRESENT MOMENT**

Inhale Dreams.

Exhale Fears.

I

am

worthy.

I
deserve
happiness.

# I am
## Present

I am
resilient.

I love my
_skin_

My Black is royal

*Today*
I WILL
ACCOMPLISH
GREATNESS

I am

myself.

I am
**FREE**
of worry

I WAS BORN WORTHY
OF

*love*

*I do not require*
THE APPROVAL OF OTHERS

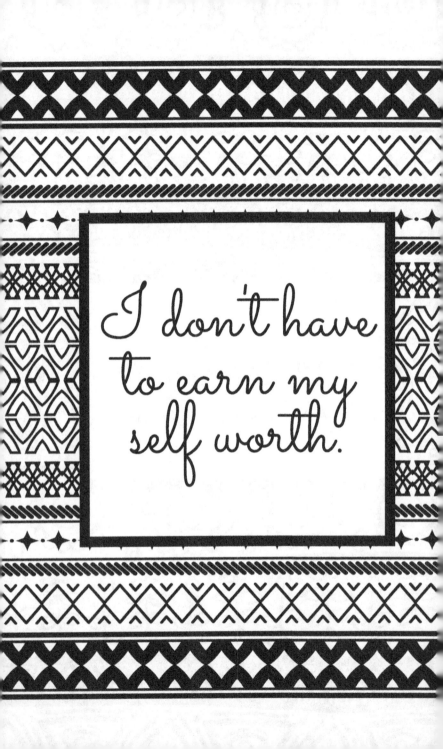

I don't have to earn my self worth.

I

---

**FORGIVE**

---

myself

The more I love myself

**THE MORE I CAN LOVE OTHERS**

# I AM DEEPLY LOVABLE

*[just the way I am]*

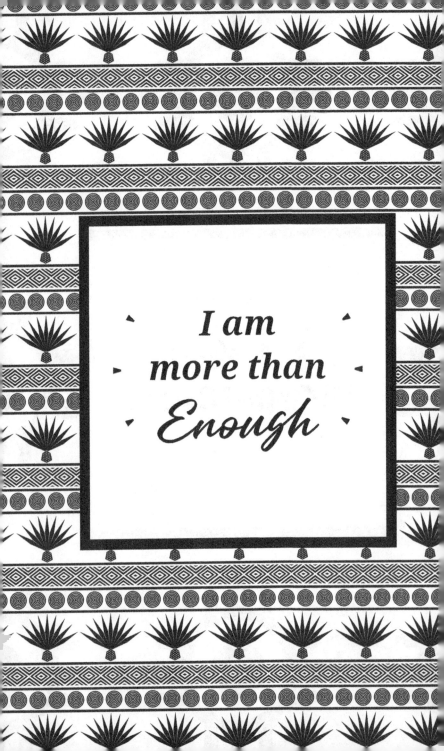

ALL I NEED IS
[already]
WITHIN ME

I am
filled and
nourished
by love

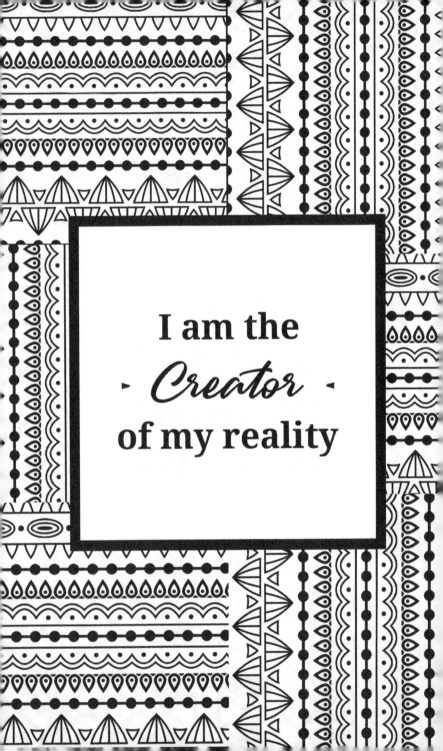

I am the

*Creator*

of my reality

I choose to be

*Positive*

I am the
Goddess

# I AM
black excellence

I own my magic

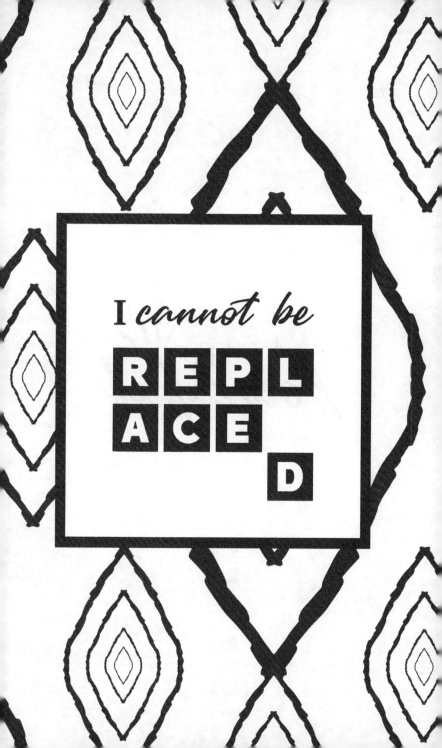

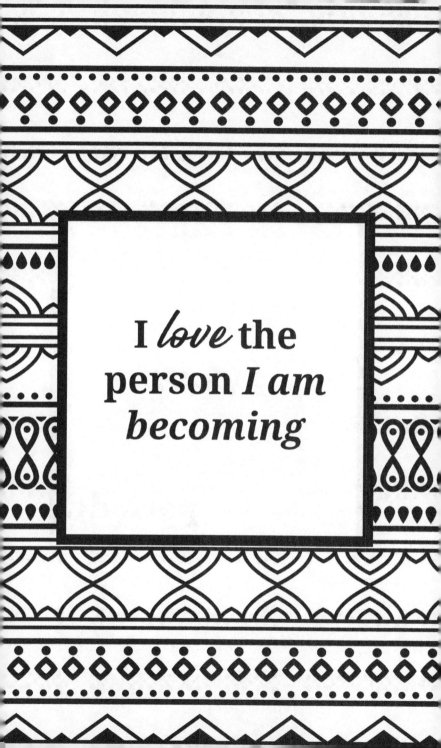

I *love* the person *I am* *becoming*

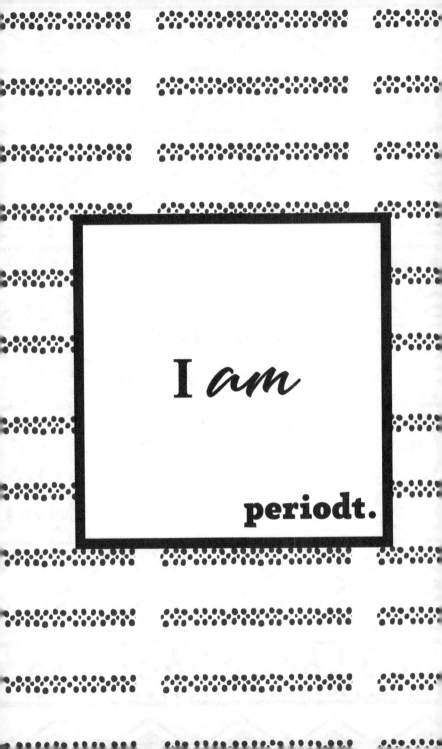

I *am*

**periodt.**

Made in the USA
Las Vegas, NV
19 March 2024